A PRIMER:

COMMUNITIES IN COLLABORATIVE CONVERSATIONS

Relationships…Possibilities…Transformation

A Primer: Communities In Collaborative Conversations

Primer: Communities in Collaborative Conversations

Copyright © 2022 by Dr. G.L Kesling

All rights reserved. No part of this book may be reproduced or used in any manner without written permission of the copyright owner except for the use of quotations in a book review.

Thank you for buying an authorized edition of this book and for complying with copyright laws by not reproducing, scanning, or distributing any part of it in any form without permission. You are supporting writers and their hard work by doing this.

ISBN: ___ 979-8-218-07115-8

ISBN: ___ 978-1-0879-8267-0

First Edition: Month, 2022

A Primer: Communities In Collaborative Conversations

TABLE OF CONTENTS

Acknowledgements 4

Biography 5

Introduction 6

    Community Engagement 6

    Paradigm Change 8

    Connectedness and Social Capital 8

    Culture, economy, governance and infrastructure: integrating four realms 10

    Understanding the Significance of Community 12

    Community engagement 14

Communities in Collaborative Conversations 17

    What CnCs Looks Like 17

    APPLICATIONS 18

    What Does It Mean? 19

        1. Community of Knowledge 20

        2. Arrangement for the Conversation 20

        3. Setting Genuine Expectation 21

        4. Attributes of the Conversation Facilitator 21

        5. Reflective Listeners 22

        6. Conversationalists Ground Rules 23

        7. Responsibilities of the Scribe 24

Appendix 26

    A. Open ended exploration 26

    B. Navigating a Community Narrative 26

        Community Narrative 26

    C. Selecting a location for Community Conversation 27

References 29

Additional Resources 33

ACKNOWLEDGEMENTS

Never doubt that a small group of thoughtful, committed, citizens can change the world. Indeed, it is the only thing that ever has.

Margaret Mead (1901-1978)

BIOGRAPHY

Dr. Kesling is a health care executive, academician, and clinician with over four decades of experience across a broad range of organizations in both the public and private sector working with local, state and federal agencies. Half of those years in collaborating, promoting and nurturing in academic environments serving as a faculty at academic health science centers' Schools of Medicine, Nursing and Health Professions.

Dr. Kesling is the founder and CEO of Catalyst Consulting, providing population behavioral health consultations.

INTRODUCTION

Everyone deserves the opportunity to live a healthy life, regardless of where they live. It might be said that a person's census-track code number has greater influence on their long-term health than their genetic code. The poor health inequities in communities are exhibited by such conditions, such as income levels, discrimination, housing stability, access to nutritious food, neighborhood safety, public education, economic opportunity, and more.

Social factors, both contextual (e.g., poverty, housing, education) and interpersonal (e.g., marginalization, social support, stigma) are important contributors to health outcomes for all people. Understanding how these factors influence health, both individually and in combination, can lead to the development and implementation of microcommunity resiliency.

Decades of research on the human stress response, both experimental and observational in method, have produced a wealth of knowledge that is directly relevant to understanding the human capacity to adapt to a wide variety of stressful events and situations. Beyond the individual, resilience can be approached at the level of communities, cities, regions or nations. Resilience at this scale concerns not only the population affected, but also, the environment in which their resilience is tested. The significance of this concept is that people are not the primary focus for resilient outcomes, but are instead, part of a wider system of interdependent factors. Community cohesion, neighborhood social capital and integration can be highlighted as key features of resilient places, while reduced social capital and cohesion can be seen as sources of vulnerability

This primer will increase the awareness, knowledge, and understanding of issues related to behavioral, psychological, and structural factors that contribute to understanding population health and health inequities. Conceptual issues, key to working towards achieving health equity to reduce health disparities at multiple levels of influence, is presented as communities in collaborative conversations so as to practice cultural humility with deliberative dialogues and co-constructed outcomes.

The purpose of the primer is to provide a different lens into the topic of resilience at the intersection of microcommunites and chronic experienced life events of the people who live there, and a process that co-creates new microcommunites.

COMMUNITY ENGAGEMENT

Community engagement has been advanced as a useful strategy for improving people's health, and as a means of enabling people who lack power to gain control over their lives – and thereby, improve their own health. Critically, true community empowerment needs to begin within the community. Various models of community engagement have been advanced. The following captures the general principles:

Outreach	Consult	Involve	Collaborate	Shared Leadership
Some Community Involvement

Communication flows from one to the other, to inform

Provides community with information.

Entities coexist.

Outcomes: Optimally, establishes communication channels and channels for outreach. | More Community Involvement

Communication flows to the community and then back, answer seeking

Gets information or feedback from the community.

Entities share information.

Outcomes: Develops connections. | Better Community Involvement

Communication flows both ways, participatory form of communication

Involves more participation with community on issues.

Entities cooperate with each other.

Outcomes: Visibility of partnership established with increased cooperation. | Community Involvement

Communication flow is bidirectional

Forms partnerships with community on each aspect of project from development to solution.

Entities form bidirectional communication channels.

Outcomes: Partnership building, trust building. | Strong Bidirectional Relationship

Final decision making is at community level.

Entities have formed strong partnership structures.

Outcomes: Broader health outcomes affecting broader community. Strong bidirectional trust built. |

Increasing Level of Community Involvement, Impact, Trust, and Communication Flow →

Reference: Modified by the authors from the International Association for Public Participation.

SOURCE: HTTPS://WWW.ATSDR.CDC.GOV/COMMUNITYENGAGEMENT/

1. Theories of change for personal involvement. Engagement with communities or members of micro-communities in strategies for development of services by empowering individuals and their active engagement with service professionals to result in sustainable changes over time.
2. Theories of change for peer-/lay-delivered interventions. The aim of empowering people by enhancing their skills is to effect sustainable change amongst themselves and their peers. Peer coaching or mentoring usually involves individuals working with a specific population on a less structured basis providing emotional support and serving as a role model (Joseph, 2001). Community Health Workers (CHW) are individuals who live in the same community and share the same cultural background, values, and customs as the target patient population (Witmer, et al., 1995). CHWs have an integral role in this type of community delivered invention model to encourage primary prevention principles to previously underserved populations.
3. Theories of empowerment to reduce health inequalities. When people are engaged in a program of community development, an empowered community is the outcome sought by enhancing their mutual support and their collective action to mobilize resources of their own and from elsewhere to make changes within the community. By involving people in identifying and defining their own health problems, this approach is most likely to develop sustainable solutions that work for both individuals and communities. It has been the focus of a growing body of literature (Minkler and Wallerstein 2008).

PARADIGM CHANGE

This text presents the findings from a synthesis that examined the theory underpinning factors involved in models of change and evidence for community engagement in terms of its influences on a wide range of health outcomes associated with community resilience. (Kesling, 2021)

The definitions, needs, and motivations of communities provide a foundation to structure on how community engagement is developed and delivered. Where community engagement is a key part of the strategy, members of the stakeholder community can be involved in the design of an intervention. Conversely, where there is less community engagement and more emphasis on interventions, members may simply be observers in its delivery.

Resilience refers to the ability to withstand stress and challenge. The concept has become subject to new interest and attention in current times. Traditionally, the focus evolves around preparedness – mitigating apparent vulnerability to events, such as pandemics, extreme weather, terrorism or catastrophic, and sometimes chronic experienced life events (CELE).

The American Psychological Association (APA) defines resilience as "the process of adapting well in the face of adversity, trauma, tragedy, threats or significant sources of stress — such as family and relationship problems, serious health problems or workplace and financial stressors. It means 'bouncing back' from difficult experiences." It is not the same as being impervious to stress. It is the capacity to recover and adapt following a stressful event.

(https://www.apa.org/helpcenter/road-resilience)

Transformatively, resilience needs to go beyond traditional definitions to arrive at a meaning of resilience for "tota civitas" (the whole community).

CONNECTEDNESS AND SOCIAL CAPITAL

Influenced by the fields of community development and sociology, social models of resilience are concerned with a community's ability to reshape thinking and action, both in planning for, and in response to internal and external factors. This view of resilience puts people at the center, and as compared with the urbanist perspective, focuses on social explanations for resilience.

Landau and Weaver describe community resilience as a community's capacity to "withstand major trauma and loss, overcome adversity, and to prevail, usually with increased resources, competence and connectedness"; that is to say, an approach for simultaneously creating a supportive environment for health and increasing the community's capacity for adaptation to stressors (Landau and Weaver, 2006 cited in Bajayo, 2010; p2). A community's belief in their own collective ability to adapt and thrive has been highlighted as a key characteristic of resilient places (Mguni and Caistor-Arendar, 2012), pointing to the centrality of culture as well as infrastructural considerations.

The character of connections between individuals within communities is an enabling aspect of resilience. Community cohesion, neighbor social capital and integration have been highlighted as key features of pre-event resilience (see, for example, Pelling, 2003; Edwards, 2009; Bajayo, 2010). Declining social capital and cohesion can be seen as fragilities that accompany the rapid growth or conservation stage of the panarchic model (Gunderson and Holling, 2003) in their book titled "Panarchy: Understanding Transformations in Systems of Humans and Nature." The essential focus of Panarchy is to rationalize the interplay between change and persistence between the predictable and unpredictable. As Putman described in 'Bowling Alone' (Putnam, 2000): "Creating (or recreating) social capital is no simple task. (p402)"

Different varieties of social capital need to be recognized as offering different types of protection and assurance. These forms of capital have been categorized as 'bonding,' 'bridging' and 'linking' (Woolcock, 1998; Halpern, 2005).

Bonding capital describes relationships grounded in similar outlooks and values and is a source of social support at a level close to the individual. Bridging capital represents links to different outlooks, views and experiences, and linking capital represents links to institutional power, such as those gained through participation in local decision-making or by having access to power elites.

Bonding capital is beneficial in providing support for and recognition of one's outlook, thereby bolstering sense of coherence. In providing social support, bonding capital can be an important resource for assisting an individual's return to pre-crisis functioning ('bouncing back') in circumstances where restoring such a set of conditions is possible. However, the absence of bridging capital leads to fragility. Granovetter's work on 'weak ties' (a cognate of bridging capital) found such ties useful for successful responses to the crisis of unemployment, i.e., finding new work (Granovetter, 1974; 1983).

Bridging capital is, therefore, important when resilience of the transformative variety is required ('bouncing beyond') as a return to pre-crisis conditions becomes impossible (for example, when a work-role or industry no longer exists).

The relationship between bridging capital and resilience at a community level lies in provision of "the patchwork of ideas, action and exercises" (Edwards, 2009) which offer options and possibilities to both individuals and their networks and communities. These 'ideas' offer the raw material for developing creative responses to unanticipated problems. Communities strong in bridging capital have the potential to administer appropriate and timely responses to shocks – a capability which can be dampened by the over-centralization of responses. Kawachi describes collective efficacy as, "the ability of residents to organize and engage in collective action" (Kawachi, 2010; p167) – in the aftermath of the 1995 Kobe earthquake in Japan. The presence of community development associations (forms of bridging capital) accelerated rescue operations and helped maintain social cohesion post-crisis (cited in Morgan et al., 2010).

Linking capital represents links to leadership and opportunity. When present, it allows a two-way flow of information between the 'grassroots or 'periphery' to the 'top' or 'center' where decision-making, resource allocation and strategic planning is located. This allows attendant knowledge of emerging threats, potential solutions and unreleased capacity to flow from one to the other. The report 'The Ownership State' (Blond, 2009) provides an outline of how governance structures could be configured to promote linking capital. Inspired in part by shared ownership models by reducing the distance and distinction between the 'frontline' or 'periphery' and the 'center' of planning, responses to intelligence can be quicker, via more distributed decision-making. That is without active and vocal engagement from citizens, making clear what they want from the public sector and taking an active role in its delivery, services will be unresponsive to users' needs, and the burden of care will increase as problems multiply.

Engaging providers and recipients multiplies the effect of individual action and changes group behavior and social outcome. It enables ordinary people to make a difference by giving government the tools to realize the actions and concerns of its citizens, it takes out the costs and burdens of ineffective management and promotes self-organization and social transformation.

CULTURE, ECONOMY, GOVERNANCE AND INFRASTRUCTURE: INTEGRATING FOUR REALMS

Building resilience at levels larger than the individual requires attention to four functional areas: culture, the economy, infrastructure and governance. The activities here need to be integrated and although, unavoidably, these actions will be taken within the professional and practical responsibilities of each domain, so the policies and planning are taken to align these constructs. Foremost to a philosophy of resilience is the promoting of key characteristics which support resilient responses; flexibility, diversity and active participation so as to support transformation and adaptation when challenges to "current state" are presented.

In the domain of culture, opportunities for participation view individuals as producers as well as consumers of cultural output allow a diversity of narratives and different forms of meaning-making to enter the framing of a larger collective understanding. As well as promoting the appreciation of diverse perspectives and values; these various stories can become the raw source material for creating new ways of being when some type of stressors threatens traditional patterns of living. Further, involvement in the production of such narratives can also promote networking and skill development to promote social inclusion. In this framework, conversations undertake the quality of a certain kind of potentially transformative communication. Through multiple iterations of interaction, participants become engaged in a unique setting where experiencing conversations as numerous dynamic co-relationships; each participant then becomes open to gaining access to helpful and self-chosen co-created alternatives in perspective.

The economy is often neglected in population health perspectives. A community can be defined in many different ways. In addition to geographical boundaries, they may also be defined by economic characteristics, interests, values, or traditions. Such communities (i.e., those with a shared identity, or a shared lived life experience) typically become the focus of the majority of the community engagement interventions (these types of asymmetries in economical and geographical identifiers between different cultural groups have led to some to different levels of social polarization). Communities are more likely to define themselves as such, or they might be defined by people outside the community, often labeling a population as monolithic. This reflects some semantic differences in how communities are perceived, both by themselves and by external organizations. This distinction between the term "population" (externally defined) and "community" (self-identified).

Other needs may also be identified differently (Bradshaw, 1972):

- A felt need, which is one directly identified by community members themselves.
- An expressed need, which is inferred by observing a community's use of services.
- A comparative need, derived by comparing service use in a similar community; or
- A normative need; derived by comparing measures of living conditions with a society norm or standard, often set by experts.

This taxonomy delineates different forms of need, which are conceptualized as being on a continuum that moves in stages away from expressly prevailing recognized models (felt need) towards an objective construct (normative need).

The way in which community engagement activities takes place (i.e., the "process" of engagement) may influence how well that activity ultimately impacts on desired outcomes. Several examples of process issues include:

- Clearly defined target groups, objectives, interventions and program components (Hamer M, Box V. 2000);
- Adequate time for community members and other stakeholders to build relationships with one another, so that they can agree a 'level playing field' in terms of language, negotiation and collegial working skills (Anastacio J, et. al 2000).
- Learning of funding sources and developing skills to build for future sources of funding (Newman J, et. al 2004).
- The degree of collective decision-making.
- Planning for on-going simple communication between participants and providers (Jemmott LS, et al 1998) and between the community engagement group and the wider community (Hamer M, Box V. 2000);
- Adequate participant and provider skills training.
- The amount and quality of organizational support required to ensure smooth project running.
- Activity timing, duration and frequency

Governance requirements for resilient systems echoes this need to allow space for different forms of individual meaning-making in conjunction with institutional requirements for accountability at both macro and micro levels. Flattened hierarchical structures or diffused decision-making promotes the integration of what become workable within local situations and can offer the wider system sources of transformation in navigating multiple agendas. The challenge for current governance conventions will be to accept a more participatory model of governance. A culture of learning will also be difficult to promote when risk aversion and standardization of procedures are the guiding viewpoints.

From a planning perspective, infrastructure is a key starting point for appraising the resilience of communities because it must support the resilience of the communities it serves.

Thinking about infrastructure at a community scale can facilitate ways of living, which allow the interactions that support the development of social capitals, networks that are stronger and more diverse, and the cross-pollination of ideas and narratives about those places, making them more resilient as a result.

UNDERSTANDING THE SIGNIFICANCE OF COMMUNITY

A community consists of a population carrying on a collective life through a set of formal and informal arrangements. Common interests and norms of conduct are implied in this definition. Of the many meanings of community, two continue to be widely used. One use of the word community is to refer to a grouping of people who live close to one another and are united by common interests and reciprocated aid. In this sense, a community is small numerically, consisting of, at most, a few hundred people, and the connotation is one of solidarity. On the other hand, the term may be used in the broader sense to refer to any population that carries on its daily life through a common set of foundations. In this sense, it may apply to a population aggregate of any size in which the members participate within a particular socio-dynamic system. Cairns (1979) research indicated that individuals who frequently interact together tend to synchronize their behavior in a way that supports both the behavior and the relationship dynamics. Cairns recognized three forms of social synchrony. The first is imitation; where the individual behavior is modeled after another individual. The second is reciprocity; where two individuals respond and react to on another in similar ways, which then reinforces the common behaviors. The third is complementarity; which occurs when two individuals have different status and behaviors, however the behaviors of each depends on that of the other (i.e., a leader-follower).

Whether used in a micro sense or in a macro sense, community commonly refers to a territorially bounded social group. The geographic area may range from a few neighboring residents on a single street to a sector of the city in the case of a micro community, and from the local city through the metropolitan area to the region in the case of a macro community. As a topographical reference, the term tends to be open-ended.

It also should be noted, however, that community is used increasingly to refer to interest groups whose common activities are relatively independent of location factors. The source of the common interest may be artistic or technical, commercial or governmental, religious or ethnic. Through this lens, a community is united by emotive bonds and that this is an important feature of commonality which then contributes to its collective identity.

The multiple meanings of community reflect the changing lifestyles that result from the ongoing processes of suburbanization. The pattern of human transactions from which a sense of community derives is growing in scope and complexity and changing in content.

Housing areas vary as much or more in racial, ethnic, and socioeconomic composition; in lifestyles; in the physical features that can be used to create images and boundaries; and in claims to a distinct character or identity.

A "model" community offers its citizens a wide selection of services and opportunities-stores, amusements, public and private services in such areas as education and medical care, and so forth. Specialists of all kinds are congregated in the larger metropolitan areas, and large populations tend to generate a variety of occupational and common-interest groups among which individuals may pick and choose. Most urban residents are able to benefit from the array of opportunities. However, some elements of the urban population find it difficult to take advantage of these opportunities; they suffer from a relative deprivation of choices.

Access and accessibility have a number of dimensions. One is physical accessibility-the capacity for getting directly in contact with persons or activities. Another is social-psychological-cumulative experiences that enable the individual to utilize and navigate the complex urban environment. A third is income, which influences where one lives, what one can afford to do, and what travel mode is at one's disposal.

Accessibility in the context of community setting has been undergoing significant changes in recent decades. Expectations and consumption patterns of residents have become polarized over the last decade and continue escalate. From the point of view of the individual and the population generally, "community" represents a shared environment. Within this environment, discretionary opportunities, creates an effective environment. Gans (1968, p. 6) has defined the effective environment as "that version of the potential environment that is manifestly or latently adopted by users," in other words, that part of the environment that the individual either actively uses or sees as available to them (or not and acts as a constraint). More contemporarily an "effective environment" may be reflective of fiscal and social inequities perpetuating a mismatch between resources and needs on an order-of-magnitude scale.

Microcommunities - Non-monolithic or homogeneous

Microcommunities, of course, differ substantially in terms of the average incomes (work-life experiences), educational levels, and ethnic compositions of their populations. These differences affect access to goods and services and thus the scale and scope of connections in the microcommunity. However, in neighborhoods with prevailing health disparities (populations at high-risk and underserved), including racial and ethnic minorities, the locus of need is paramount and traditional approaches to address these needs have been ineffective.

Micro-communities are characteristic of human relationships. What the micro-community's current -state and what it will be in the future, both result from decisions made by people interacting, negotiating, and working together. Trust and deep relationships are crucial to holding micro-communities together year after year and making resilience durable—but they can be challenging to build.

COMMUNITY ENGAGEMENT

The process of engaging communities in dialogues and decision-making about how to best achieve long-term improvements and impact — is a core part of developing population health and sustainability. Leveraging local knowledge and expertise at the micro-community level can create better policy development and program planning.

On January 31, 2020, the U.S. Secretary of Health and Human Services (HHS) issued a declaration of a public health emergency related to COVID-19 and mobilized the Operating Divisions of HHS. On March 13, 2020, the President declared a national emergency in response to COVID-19. In addition, the WHO declared the novel coronavirus a pandemic on March 11, 2020.

The COVID-19 pandemic highlighted the magnitude of social, racial and health injustice and inequity in communities. Marginalized and minoritize populations disproportionately experienced the acute distress of the pandemic and it only exacerbated long-standing sociodemographic inequities in micro-communities. While everyone is at risk for COVID-19, individuals who have underlying medical conditions are at higher risk for severe illness from COVID-19. In addition, people of color disproportionately have higher rates of many chronic conditions, such as diabetes, hypertension, kidney disease, and asthma, which are associated with the social determinants of health. Furthermore, people of color are overrepresented in certain sections in communities. This pandemic is revealing the consequences of these longstanding inequities and the urgent need to advance micro-community level resilience and prevent further exacerbating disparities.

Post-COVID-19, the challenge will be to frame the view that population health disparities can be addressed, and progress is possible and will be successful when shared outcomes are defined, collective action is aligned, and local improvement efforts are co-led by policymakers, stakeholders, and community members most impacted by the decisions being made.

Fundamental questions remain pertaining to the building of resilient micro- communities. How should the characteristics of resilient be identified?

What are the characteristics of the resilience that make it adaptable to the risks? How could these resilient characteristics be expressed in sustainable resilient micro- community practices? Answering these questions are important on the micro-community level because the specific strategies and effective ways for each distinctively identify how micro-communities will deal with risks, how they should be delineated, thus, guiding the integrated social–ecological systems in which communal systems and ecosystems are acknowledged as interdependent, and coevolving.

In essence, the social-ecological systems approach emphasizes that people, communities, economies, societies, cultures are embedded parts of the environment and shape it, from local to global scales. At the same time people, communities, economies, societies, cultures are shaped by, dependent on, and evolving with the environment (Clark and Munn 1986, Folke et al. 2011, Leach et al. 2012). Therefore, people are not just inhabitants of the micro-community, but their interactions all together is shaping resilience (or not) in diverse ways, consciously or unconsciously.

Although substantive progress has been made through various studies in the resilient urban community practices, the academics have not reached an agreement on what are the characteristics of resilience. Wildavsky (1990) proposed six characteristics of a resilient system, namely; homeostasis, omnivory, high flux, flatness, buffering and redundancy. Based on this, Wardekker, Jong, Knoop, & Sluijs (2010) considered 'foresight and preparedness/planning,' 'compartmentalization' and 'flexible planning/design' as practical principles for urban resilience. Ahern, Qin, & Liu (2011) argued for five urban planning and design strategies to achieve urban resilience, including multifunctionality, redundancy and modularization, (biological and social) diversity, multiscale networks and connectivity, and adaptive planning and design. They also considered resilient community to have eight major features, including diversity, allowing for variability, modularity, innovation, tight feedbacks, overlap in governance, social capital and ecosystem services (Ahern et al., 2011).

In addition, other similar or relevant terms of describing urban resilience characteristics are often discussed in the literature, including 'the ability to learn(Newman, 2009), 'self-(re)organizing ability' (Carpenter, Walker, Anderies, & Abel, 2001; Tompkins & Adger, 2004), action, 'recovery' (Meerow, Newell, & Stults, 2016), flexibility, 'robustness' (Wardekker et al., 2010), autonomy, 'interdependence' (Brody, Godschalk, & Burby, 2003), 'reflexivity and connectivity' (Davoudi & Strange,2009). As discussed above, the literature generally shows ambiguous and uncertain understandings of the characteristics of resilience.

The intangible concept of community resilience needs to be understood and realized through more tangible dimensions by building a resilient micro-community model, therefore, the dimensions which express the characteristics of resilience can be expressed. It is helpful to clarify the target object of community resilience building. The physical environment is on the fundamental layer of the resilient micro-community model, including two performance dimensions of the resilient characteristics: the first is the spatial pattern of traffic roads, residential buildings, activity sites (services) and degree of urban blight in the community, and the second is the infrastructure for living and municipal public utilities, municipal network, information and communication. These two dimensions are the functional support of the whole resilient micro-community and the assurance for dealing with all kinds of biopsychosocial indices.

Narratives must be discernable to both individuals and communities through times of change as a component of the glue that holds social networks together. Re-storying – the ability for new stories to be created, told and heard about communities and individuals in a manner salient to their histories and biographies; therefore, it becomes a key characteristic of communities and societies to support both individual and collective resilience. The ways in which these events are understood and interpreted, however, makes a considerable difference to their operationalization.

David Epston and Michael White introduced the narrative metaphor and the reauthoring metaphor to the therapeutic field (Epston & White 1990; Epston 1992; White 2001). One of the key considerations that their work introduced was to consider how stories shape people's identities. In turn this led to an exploration of what makes up a story. There are four elements that go into the development of a storyline. Re-authoring is comprised of: i) events, ii) in a sequence, iii) across time, iv) organized according to a plot or theme. (Epston & White 1990; Epston 1992; White 2001).

The re-authoring conversations map divides the questions that are explored into two categories. One category involves questions that inquire about the 'landscape of action' and the other category involves questions that inquire about the 'landscape of identity' (Bruner 1986; Epston & White 1990; White 1995).

Landscape of action questions involve inquiries into events and actions.

We are always interested in inviting people to speak about their identities in terms of 'intentional states' because this makes story-making more possible. If we try to find out the values, hopes and dreams that are guiding someone's actions, there are ways to trace the history of these, to link them to the hopes and dreams of other people, and to forecast what future actions will flow from these commitments. Intentional states of identity include –

- Intentions or purposes,
- Values / beliefs,
- Hopes and dreams.
- Principles for living and
- Commitments

Landscape of identity questions encourage people to explore a different territory.

They relate to the implications that this alternative storyline has in terms of the person's understanding of their identity. Landscape of identity questions invite people to reflect differently on their own identities and the identities of others.

We are interested in exploring the intentions, hopes, values and commitments that shape people's actions rather than any internal deficits or deficiencies, or for that matter any internal 'resources,' 'strengths' or 'qualities'

The ways in which we engage with our commitments, purposes, beliefs, values and dreams shape our actions and how we live our lives. Inviting people to think about these intentional states and linking them to alternative storylines (formed from unique outcomes) provides a fertile ground for re-authoring conversations.

Michael White describes a 'hierarchy' of these intentional states (White 2003). It seems that it is easier for people to respond to questions about intentional states if we start by asking questions about:

- Their intentions or purposes that shaped a particular action,
- Then ask about the values and beliefs that are supporting these,
- Then the hopes and dreams that are associated with these values,
- Then the principles of living that are represented by those hopes and dreams,
- And finally, the commitments, or what it is that people stand-up for in life.

Central to this work with micro-communities is a consideration of our language, and the narratives that shape our thinking. Narratives are embedded in the structure of communities. Narratives shape what questions we ask and what solutions we might develop. They even shape our descriptions of the situation, what attributes are projected upon community and situations are emphasized through dominant narratives influence our understanding of what we deem possible and not possible.

COMMUNITIES IN COLLABORATIVE CONVERSATIONS

Communities in Collaborative Conversations provides an operative framework to facilitate dialog across a wide array of small and large groups and organizations (voluntary, governmental, private, not-for-profit, NGO, etc.).

Communities in Collaborative Conversations (CnCs) may function at various levels; highly active and experiential in its articulations, so as to bring intra and extra group diverse perspectives on real life and the processes of "lived life experiences."

It may be conceptualized as both a model and an approach where the conjectural and rational aspects interconnectedness for strengthening relationships, building an environment of mutual trust and understanding. The processes and format developed through CnCs uniquely and effectively serve as a "dynamic think tank" for bringing together people who hold in-common matters of similar concern and finding the means of addressing important unmet needs.

CnCs develops a new kind of community that is co-created in conversation. Individuals, groups or organizations have historically labeled these types of meeting, interactions, and committees as "issues" or "problems" directed. The practices of CnCs engages not only the participants present, but others who become informed and aware of the conversational processes that is inclusive of the invited others. This engagement is completely new, it is generative, and it leads to unimagined possibilities for all. It becomes more than a conversational process that identifies, encourages and honors the time and space for speaking and listening, it is the "never before experienced" that reinforces opportunity for transformation.

WHAT CNCS LOOKS LIKE

Envision people meeting; in conversation together; having Socratic inquiry-based and authentic dialogue focused on discovering together because they hold in common some matter of importance, some need not fully met. What is different here is they are now a new community, and they are about to become participants in a new kind of conversation.

This new community is composed of three groups of participants: conversationalists, reflective listeners and conversational facilitators. For example, there are twenty people who have come together for their first meeting. The first of the three groups are twelve conversationalists or group participants in traditional group meetings/sessions. They will sit and talk together (optimally in a circle). Their conversation will be overheard by a second group of six reflective listeners. This second group listens to and reflects among themselves on their experience of the conversation performed by the first group. The final two participants are off to the side, so as not to be overtly noticed. They are called conversation facilitators because their role is keeping the conversation going, without necessarily directing it.

The narrative process fosters the creation of an atmosphere of active involvement and relationships. These interactions form a unique flow for the participants to engage in making meaning. There is a valuing of the person and the personal experiences and views, moreover, inviting people to feel truly involved.

In this new dynamic group community, there are communicators and facilitators engaged in conversations while the reflectors listen. After a time, this first conversation pauses so that the conversationalists and facilitators can listen as the reflectors share their thoughts with one another.

This second conversation, among the community of reflectors, focuses on discovering and making public inner thoughts and feelings. The reflectors ask and address the question: "What do we think and feel about the conversation we have just experienced?" There is the exploration of micro-narratives. These can be conceptualized as subscenarios or substories.

When the reflectors pause, the conversationalist and facilitators respond among themselves to what they heard; things the reflectors said that catch their curiosity and engage them in further conversation.

There may be several rounds of conversation and then reflections. It is important to notice that the conversational processes developed in this format enable participants to identify invited others; that is those not now present now but whose future participation would be helpful.

In summary these are the fundamental aspects of CnC:

- Processes that create new communities in conversation
- Sponsoring and expanding relationships
- The possibility of preferred transformations.

While individual variation may be necessary, generally the composition of each of the three groups optimally functions with sixty percent conversationalists, thirty percent reflective listeners and ten percent conversational facilitators.

APPLICATIONS

The importance of the theoretical and philosophical aspects is prominent in strengthening relationships, building an environment of mutual trust and understanding. The value of this new developmental knowledge to participants (collaborators) cannot be underestimated.

This approach emphasizes the sensitivity to the fact that individuals grow and change over time and that their capacities and concerns may transform over their life course.

Communities in Collaborative Conversation can provide a different approach to improving the lives of individuals, families, organizations and society.

WHAT DOES IT MEAN?

Micro-communities are representative of human relationships. What the micro-community's current-state and what it will be in the future, both result from decisions made by people interacting, negotiating, and working together. Trust and deep relationships are crucial to holding micro-communities together year after year and making resilience durable—but they can be challenging to build.

Resilience building must be cognizant of the political and economic processes that determine what gets done, how it gets done, who decides, and who benefits. People of all interests and means must be able to participate in and benefit from resilience building; indeed, if there is to be true resilience, micro-communities must embrace dissent and diversity.

The goals of micro-community resilience-building efforts are best set by and focused on the needs of the people who make up that specific community—not just the requests of the most governmentally engaged or external stakeholders. Also, community members must collectively have power and responsibility for cultivating the resilience of their micro-community as active participants and leaders—rather than only as observers.

Community resilience building is not an engineering problem solvable just by knowledge and skill. It is a social undertaking, involving thousands or even millions of conversations and meaningful relationships, hopes, and fears. It confronts us and compels us to engage with people with whom we may disagree—perhaps would have never known.

We need motivation and emotional strength to take on such personally challenging work. Individuals need courage to speak out about their views and needs and make themselves personally vulnerable. Micro-communities, too, need courage to create space for difficult conversations, make far-reaching investments and policy changes, and risk sharing political and economic power. Courage is the ability to do something one knows is difficult and building micro-community resilience in the face of historical, prevailing and at time unimageable barriers can be difficult indeed. Foundation for Communities in Conversation.

Community centered Conversations serve two important purposes:

- The conversations and style of dialogue is a way to authentically engage members of the community.
- A Community of Knowledge begins to develop that informs a different type decision-making in numerous ways.

Community engagement so as to better to understand:

- Both individual and a collective understanding of the aspirations for the community.
- Insightfulness into concerns.
- Representations of how individuals think and talk about a given issue in relation to the community.
- The adaptations needed to reach the aspirations for the community.
- Exploration of the range and scale of possibilities and the type of relationships to support action taking.

Community engagement Conversation "stories" to inform:

- Engagement within the community: Attractive new individuals invites new relationships.
- Discovery of new cohorts: Sharing the Community of Knowledge creates coalition opportunities.
- Emerging strategies: Constructing a new and different capacity to work together.
- Rallying resources: Creating natural pathways for people to contribute.

1. COMMUNITY OF KNOWLEDGE

The value of a Community of Knowledge:

- Understanding these communities (or micro-societies) requires an awareness of who is included and who is excluded, as well as what factors are used to make the decisions about who belongs.
- Articulates the foundation of work and decisions in what matters to the population.
- Focuses on key issues and related connections in verbally how language is representative of how people communicate.
- Learning a sense of common purpose.
- Empowers setting representative goals.
- Enriches the conversations about choices so the work is more pertinent and has greater impact.
- Recognizes communities construct a Community of Knowledge.

2. ARRANGEMENT FOR THE CONVERSATION

The ideal size for these conversations is between 8 and 15 individuals who are the "Conversationalist." There will be 4 to 6 "reflective listeners" and 1 or 2 "conversation facilitators." To get that many, invite at least 20 people, as some will be unable to make it. If fewer than 8 show up, that's fine. Go ahead. It'll be worth time to begin this new style of interactions. If more than 20 shows up, consider breaking into two groups.

Decide whom to invite

These conversations are a powerful way to get to know different parts of the community or learn from new and never heard from voices. Consider what is needed, essential or critical to learn. Initially is there the need to get a general understanding of how individuals see the community globally? If yes, then invite a cross-sectional group of individuals to participate. Possibly the need is to get a better sense of a specific topic or a more targeted strategy of evolving issues in a community then this may be a different cohort-representation. All possibilities are fine.

Guidelines for getting people to participate

- Personally invite and inspire their participation.
- Inquire about other individuals to invite.
- Outline clearly the type of interactions and conversations to be held.
- Follow up by email or phone to determine if there are new questions or considerations that will help the person decide to attend.

3. SETTING GENUINE EXPECTATION

When inviting people to the conversations, it is important to share clear, genuine expectations. This is very different from what individuals have participated in the past; so, it is supportive to explain what these conversations ARE and what they ARE NOT.

Primary, what are these conversations:

- Ninety-minutes to two-hour conversations that helps us better understand you and your community and co-create a knowledge based on understand the "lived experiences."
- Focused on learning. Important in strengthening relationships, building an environment of mutual trust and understanding.
- Support iterative conversations in order to generate a (possibly unbounded) sequence of outcomes.

Secondly, what these conversations are not:

- A town hall meeting ; some type of academic research or a focus group.
- Agenda "tized"
- About any one solution or approach
- A grievance session

4. ATTRIBUTES OF THE CONVERSATION FACILITATOR

THE RESPONSIBILITY OF A CONVERSATION FACILITATOR

The main responsibility of a Conversation Facilitator is to create an environment that enables individuals to learn about the community and common aspirations. It's more than just running a meeting. Good Conversation Facilitators are curious listeners, focused on creating a conversation where people can discover and learn from one another and explore their own ideas. "Making meaning" and understanding are created in relationship and conversation.

Conversation Facilitators will need to:

- Remain neutral about the topic under discussion; is not seen as having his or her own agenda or siding with one group.
- Explore ideas with individuals; displays a genuine sense of curiosity.
- Listen to individuals and build confidence.
- Encourage individuals to consider different perspectives and lived stories.
- Have experience leading or facilitating group discussions (not simply directing).
- Remain focused on the essence of having the conversation — it's about learning.
- Prepare for each new conversational session by going over individual reflective notes from previous conversations.

5. REFLECTIVE LISTENERS

"Reflective listening" is a way of listening and responding to another person that improves mutual understanding and trust. Taking a position of "not knowing" and being transparent.

Participating as a Reflective Listener has four distinctive characteristics:

First, it emphasizes conversation as a mutually and openly shared experience. Frequently, individuals may focus their attention on their intra-personal views in conversation. Active listening compensates for this tendency by emphasizing the need to focus attention on the collective other's views.

Second, reflective listening stresses an open-ended attitude toward conversation. Reflective listening utilizes modesty, humility, trust, and a vigorous recognition that others are choice-makers.

Third, in reflective listening, the parties focus on what is happening among all participants, when you are listening reflectiveally you join with all others in the process of co-creating meaning.

Finally, reflective listening focuses on the present (what we are doing now), rather than primarily on future goals (what we will do), or on past events (what we did then). Reflective listening requires that one be fully present to the process. This attitude of being-in-the-present helps each participant to unify his or her actions, intentions, and speech. It can also ameliorate power differences."

REFLECTING LISTENER TEAM PROCESS
PRE-SESSION:
The Reflective Listeners are introduced to the participants (conversationalists).

The role of the Team is to be:

- Polite and affirming

- Reflect only on what has been discussed, observed, not observed
- Focus on the positive aspects of the conversations
- Speculative, tentative, and not the expert
- Multi-person perspective orientation
- Use positive connotation
- Use common language

SESSION (THE MEETING)

The Reflective Listeners sit outside of the participants. After 45 minutes, the participants pause their conversations to hear from the Reflective Listeners.

Each member of the Team shares their observations by:

- Posing a question
- Hypothesize in an "appropriately unusual" way
- Offer an affirmation
- Offer a different perspective
- State something, they are curious about
- Talk to each other; comment on another team member's idea
- Emphasize something positive
- Positively connote a difficulty
- Notice the themes of the team's reflections

THE INTER-SESSION

After 15 to 20 minutes the Reflecting Team pauses. The participants share their thoughts and observations on the Teams' observations.

POST SESSION(S)

Shifts in Thinking: From Outputs to Outcomes

A key challenge in bringing diverse groups together is embedding outcomes to support the shift from outputs (services, things, transactions) to outcomes (intended impact).

Shifts in Thinking: From Deficits to Strengths

To broaden our understanding of 'conversations' to develop "relationships resources."

6. CONVERSATIONALISTS GROUND RULES

Conversations are based on a special kind of inter-personal interaction, in which the basic feature is that each participant feels and can be heard and respected:

- To begin and carry through
- To present
- To take action
- To shape

- To sustain a dialogue instead of a monologue

Ground Rules

1. Have a "kitchen table" conversation

To give interested participants an opportunity to learn from and share with each other, create a sense of community, and discuss options and alternatives where everyone participates; no one dominates.

2. There are no "right answers"

Draw on individual experiences, views and beliefs.

3. Maintain an open mind

Carefully listening and exploring an understanding of the views of those who may disagree

4. Sustain the core purpose of the conversations

Stick to the questions; try not to ramble.

7. RESPONSIBILITIES OF THE SCRIBE

The foremost responsibility of a Scribe is to capture key insights, ideas, themes, turning points and quotes from the Community in Collaborative Conversation. Scribes work with Conversation Facilitators to identify themes within conversations and across several conversations.

AN EFFECTIVE SCRIBE:
- Is attentive
- Is observant, noting what people say, how they say it (the emotion, tension or doubt) and even what people aren't saying (what's being ignored).
- Captures the essence of the conversation without inserting his/her own voice, words or judgment.
- Is good with details (like the specific words that people are using) AND able to help translate that into larger themes.
- Stays focused on the goal of the conversation
- Immediately after the conversation, talk with the Conversation Facilitators to compare notes. Ask:
- What were your impressions of the conversation?
- What ideas, actions or comments really seemed to resonate with the group?
- What did you notice in terms of the group's energy and emotion?
- What quotes stood out for you? What do we need to write down while it's fresh?

Key component to building trust with micro-communities to increase community engagement.

1. Continuously be transparent: Transparency is critical and a prevailing principle that must be upheld throughout the stakeholder engagement
1. process. From the initial contact and every opportunity, clearly communicate to stakeholders the objectives of the engagement process and seek to avoid over-promising actions or results where deliverability is possible. This is essential to maintaining a positive and constructive long-term relationship.
2. Partner with people to deliver change: The ability to promote and implement action lies in the critical mass of people, that brings with it diversity in culture, knowledge and innovation pivotal to developing new ideas for change action. Activity and relentlessly involving communities in the work will develop the most innovative and impactful outcome actions.
3. Enduring engagement strategies are diverse and inclusive: A variety of engagement channels must be utilized to communicate with different participants, with varying experiences and needs, while ensuring unwavering messaging. Geographic location, language, age, sex, race and socio-economic parameters and other intersectionality's of an individual or group's identity all needs to be considered in an inclusive engagement strategy.
4. Engagement is a progression, not a final end point: Community engagement should not be seen as a means to an end but should form part of a wider process of relationship building and co-developmenting practices. Build on previous community engagement and improve the relationship with a community over time. This can be accomplished through tracking, measuring and reporting on stakeholder engagement to comprehend what is effective and what is not working well.
5. Build community capacity through participation: Working with any and all communities presents challenges due to historical and evolving mistrust, misunderstanding, external agendas and quick fixes.
6. Nurturing the active involvement of the community within an Inclusive participatory engagement strategy through co-ownership and design practices, can build capacity, upskill members of the community and enable sustainable ownership in driving change action forward
7. Lead with integrity: Making sure that each and all encounters with the community collectively and people individually is led and delivered with integrity requires upholding the principles of transparency, collaboration and accessibility. This can be done through regular self-evaluation with candor.

APPENDIX

A. OPEN ENDED EXPLORATION

Exploration and an Opportunity to Collaborate

Framing initial explorations of how individuals view, experience and look to what is "different"

Aspirations (for the micro/ macro community):

Main concerns (top-of-mind concerns about the larger community):

Specific issue concerns (those concerns related to the issue individuals are exploring):

Actions that would make a difference

Who are members of my current network

B. NAVIGATING A COMMUNITY NARRATIVE

The essence of Communities in Collaborative Conversations is to try to reveal a story about what is being heard in the language that people use every day. A "thick story" combined with personal examples from Communities in Collaborative Conversations becomes a powerful combination of Communal Knowledge (a multi-perspectival view)

COMMUNITY NARRATIVE

People want (*aspirations*), but they're concerned that (*main concerns*).

As people talk more about those concerns, they talk specifically about (*Specific issue(s)*).

They believe we need to focus on (actions) and if (*groups*) played a part in those actions that folks would be more likely trust the effort and step forward.

C. SELECTING A LOCATION FOR COMMUNITY CONVERSATION

Site location can have a big impact on the success of the Community Conversation. The setting can affect who attends each session, the quality of the conversation and the group's ability to experience an environment conducive for conversations.

Essential elements to consider:

- Community focused and history of local groups use . Usually this excludes government or "official" places.
- Has adequate expansion spaces for second or third room availably depending on variable group size group.
- Has availably in the evenings and/or on weekends.
- Offers a comfortable environment.
- Is not too noisy or full of distractions.
- Is easily accessible to all participants: plenty of parking, centrally located, safe, near public transportation, accessible to those with disabilities.
- Are affordable given resources.

Scribe

Facilitators

Reflecting Team   **Conversationalist**

REFERENCES

Ahern, J., Qin, Y., & Liu, H. (2011). From fail-safe to safe-to-fail: Sustainability and resilience in the new urban world. Landscape and Urban Planning, 100(4), 341–343.

Anastacio J, Gidley B, Hart L, Keith M, Mayo M, Kowarzik U. Reflecting realities: participants' perspectives on integrated communities and sustainable development. York: Joseph Rowntree Foundation; 2000.

Bajayo R. Community Resilience: A Literature Review and Public Health Planning Framework. La Trobe University; 2010.

Blond P. The ownership state. London; NESTA/ResPublica; 2009.

Bradshaw J. A taxonomy of social need. In: McLachlan G, editor. Problems and progress in medical care seventh series Nuffield Provisional Hospitals Trust: Open University Press; 1972.

Brody, S. D., Godschalk, D. R., & Burby, R. J. (2003). Mandating citizen participation in plan making: Six strategic planning choices. Journal of the American Planning Association, 69(3), 245–264.

Bruner, J. 1986: Actual Minds, Possible Worlds. Massachusetts: Harvard University Press. Cairns, R. B. (1979). Social development: The origins and plasticity of interchanges. San Francisco, CA: W. H. Freeman

Carpenter, S., Walker, B., Anderies, J. M., & Abel, N. (2001). From metaphor to measurement: Resilience of what to what? Ecosystems, 4(8), 765–781.

Clark, W. C., and R. E. Munn, editors. 1986. Sustainable development of the biosphere. Cambridge University Press, Cambridge, UK.

Davoudi, S., & Strange, I. (2009). Conceptions of space and place in strategic spatial planning.

(172), 343-346.

Edwards C. Resilient nation. London: Demos; 2009.

Epston, D. 1992: 'A proposal for re-authoring therapy: Rose's revisioning of her life.' In McNamee, S. & Gergen, K.J. (eds): Therapy as a Social Construction. London: Sage Publications. Republished in Epston, D. 1998: Catching up with David Epston: A collection of narrative practice-based papers. Adelaide: Dulwich Centre Publications.

Epston, D. 1994: 'Expanding the conversation.' Family Therapy Networker, Nov/Dec. Republished in Epston, D. 1998: Catching up with David Epston: A collection of narrative practice-based papers. Adelaide: Dulwich Centre Publications.

Epston, D. & White, M. 1990: Narrative Means to Therapeutic Ends. New York:

W.W.Norton.

Folke, C. 1991. Socio-economic dependence on the life-supporting environment. Pages 77-94 in C. Folke and T. Kåberger, editors. Linking the natural environment and the economy: essays from the Eco-Eco Group. Kluwer Academic, Dordrecht, The Netherlands.

Epston, D. 1992: 'A proposal for re-authoring therapy: Rose's revisioning of her life.' In McNamee, S. & Gergen, K.J. (eds): Therapy as a Social Construction. London: Sage Publications.

Epston, D. & White, M. 1990: Narrative Means to Therapeutic Ends. New York: W.W.Norton.

Granovetter MS. Getting a Job: A Study of Contacts and Careers. Cambridge, MA: Harvard University Press; 1974.

Gans, H. Planning, social : I I Regional and urban. I n D. Sills (d .), International encyclopedia of the social sciences. Vol . 1 2 . pp. 1 29-1 3 7 . New York: Macmillan and Free Press, 1 968.

Granovetter M. The strength of weak ties: A network theory revisited. Sociological Theory 1983;1(1):201-233.

Gunderson, Lance and C. S. Holding. Panarchy: Understanding Transformations in Human and Natural Systems. Washington: Island Press, 2002.

Halpern D. Social Capital. Cambridge: Policy Press: 2005.

Joseph DH, Griffin M, Hall RF, Sullivan ED: Peer coaching: an intervention for individuals struggling with diabetes. Diabetes Educ 27:703–710, 2001

Kawachi, C. The relationship between health assets, social capital and cohesive communities. In: Morgan A, Davies M, Ziglio E (eds.) Health assets in a global context: theory, methods, action. New York: Springer; 2010.

Kesling, Gary, Building Sustainable Communities. 16th Annual Texas Conference on Health Disparities Community Approaches to Health Equity June 10-11, 2021, Texas Center for Health Disparities , Center for Diversity and International Programs, University of North Texas Health Science Center, Fort Worth, Texas

Landau J, Weaver AM. The LINC model of family and community resilience: New approaches to disaster response. Journal of Family and Consumer Sciences 2006;98(2):11-14.

Leach, M., J. Rockström, P. Raskin, I. Scoones, A. C. Stirling, A. Smith, J. Thompson, E. Millstone, A. Ely, E. Arond, C. Folke, and P. Olsson. 2012. Transforming innovation for sustainability. Ecology and Society 17(2):11.

Halpern D. Social Capital. Cambridge: Policy Press: 2005.

Hamer M, Box V. An evaluation of the development and functioning of the Boscombe network for change, a health alliance or partnership for health in Dorset. Health Educ J. 2000;59:238–52

Meerow, S., Newell, J. P., & Stults, M. (2016). Defining urban resilience: A review. Landscape and Urban Planning, 147, 38–49.

Mguni N, Bacon N. Taking the temperature of local communities: The Wellbeing and Resilience Measure (WARM). London: The Young Foundation; 2010.

Mguni N, Caistor-Arendar L. Rowing against the tide. Making the case for community resilience. London: The Young Foundation; 2012.

Minkler M, Wallerstein N, editors. Community-based participatory research for health: from process to outcomes. San Francisco (CA): Jossey-Bass; 2008

Morgan A, Davies M, Ziglio E. Health assets in a global context: theory, methods, action. New York: Springer; 2010.

Newman T, Yates T, Masten A. What Works in Building Resilience? Barkingside: Barnardo's; 2004.

Newman P, Beatley T, Boyer H. Resilient cities: responding to peak oil and climate change. Washington DC: Island Press; 2009.

Pelling M. The vulnerability of cities: natural disasters and resilience. Abingdon: Earthscan; 2003.

Putnam R. Bowling Alone: The Collapse and Revival of American Community. New York: Simon and Schuster; 2000.

Tompkins, E. L., & Adger, W. N. (2004). Does adaptive management of natural resources enhance resilience to climate change? Ecology Society, 9(2004), 1–14.

Wardekker, J. A., Jong, A. D., Knoop, J. M., & Sluijs, J. P. V. D. (2010). Operationalizing a resilience approach to adapting an urban delta to uncertain climate changes. Technological Forecasting Social Change, 77(6), 987–998

Witmer A, Seifer SD, Finocchio L, Leslie J, O'Neil EH: Community health workers: integral Members of the health care work force. Am J Public Health 85:1055–1058, 1995

White, M. 1995a: 'The narrative perspective in therapy', an interview by Bubenzer, D., West,

J. & Boughner, S. In Re-Authoring Lives: Interviews and essays, pp.11-40. Adelaide:

Dulwich Centre Publications. White, M. 2001a: 'The narrative metaphor in family therapy', an interview with Denborough,

D. In Denborough, D. (ed): Family Therapy: Exploring the field's past, present & possible futures. Adelaide: Dulwich Centre Publications.

White, M. 2003b: Intensive training in narrative therapy. Dulwich Centre. Unpublished

Wildavsky, A. B. (1990). Searching for safety. Journal of Risk Insurance, 57(3), 564.

Witmer A, Seifer SD, Finocchio L, Leslie J, O'Neil EH: Community health workers: integral Members of the health care work force. Am J Public Health 85:1055–1058, 1995

Woolcock M. Social capital and economic development: Toward a theoretical synthesis and policy framework. Theory and Society 1998;27(2):151-208.

ADDITIONAL RESOURCES

Aldwin C, Igarashi H. An ecological model of resilience in late life. Annual Review of Gerontology and Geriatrics 2012;32(1):115-130.

Anderson KM. Uncovering survival abilities in children who have been sexually abused. Families in Society: Journal of Contemporary Human Services 1997;78(6):592-599.

Antonovsky A. Health, stress and coping, San Francisco: Jossey-Bass Publishers; 1979

Antonovsky A. The structure and properties of the sense of coherence scale. Social Science and Medicine 1993;36(6):725-733.

Applegath JC. Future Proofing Cities: Strategies to help cities develop capacities to absorb future shocks and stresses.

Appleyard D. Livable Streets: Protected Neighborhoods? Annals of the American Academy of Political and Social Science 1980;451(1):106-117.

Arroyo CG, Zigler E. Racial identity, academic achievement, and the psychological well-being of economically disadvantaged adolescents. Journal of Personality and Social Psychology 1995;69(5):903.

Bajayo R. Community Resilience: A Literature Review and Public Health Planning Framework. La Trobe University; 2010.

Bartone P. Test-retest reliability of the dispositional resilience scale-15, a brief hardiness scale. Psychological Reports 2007;101(3 Pt 1):943-944.

Berkman LF, Kawachi I, editors. Social epidemiology. New York: Oxford University Press, 2000.

Berry JW. Acculturation: Living successfully in two cultures. International Journal of Intercultural Relations 2005;29:697-712.

Biscoe B, Harris B. Resiliency Attitudes Scale manual. Oklahoma City, Oklahoma: Eagle Ridge Institute; 1994.

Black C. Working for a Healthier Tomorrow. London: The Stationary Office; 2008.

Block J, Kremen AM. IQ and ego-resiliency: conceptual and empirical connections and separateness. Journal of Personality and Social Psychology 1996;70(2):349-361.

Blond P. The ownership state. London; NESTA/ResPublica; 2009.

Boin A, McConnell A. Preparing for critical infrastructure breakdowns: the limits of crisis management and the need for resilience Journal of Contingencies and Crisis Management 2007;15(1):50-59.

Bolger KE, Patterson CJ. Sequelae of child maltreatment: Vulnerability and resilience. In: Luthar SS (ed.) Resilience and vulnerability: Adaptation in the context of childhood adversities. Cambridge: Cambridge University Press; 2003. p156-181.

Bottrell D. Understanding 'marginal' perspectives towards a social theory of resilience. Qualitative Social Work 2009;8(3):321-339.

Boyden J, Cooper E. Questioning the power of resilience. Are children up to the task of disrupting the transmission of poverty? CPRC Working Paper 37. Manchester: Chronic Poverty Research Centre; 2007.

Bremner, J.D., Vermetten. Development and Psychopathology, 13 (2001), 473–489

A. M. Brandt, A. Botelho, Not a perfect storm—Covid-19 and the importance of language. N. Engl. J. Med. 382, 1493–1495 (2020).

Bruguglio L. Economic Vulnerability and Resilience: concepts and measurements. In: Briguglio, Eliawony, Kisamga (eds.) Economic vulnerability and resilience of small states. London: Islands and Small States Institute of the University of Malta in collaboration with the Commonwealth Secretariat; 2004.

Bruner, J. 1986: Actual Minds, Possible Worlds. Massachusetts: Harvard University Press. R. D. Bullard, B. Wright, Race, Place, and Environmental Justice after Hurricane Katrina: Struggles to Reclaim, Rebuild, and Revitalize New Orleans and the Gulf Coast (Perseus, 2009).

Burnell J. Small Change: understanding cultural action as a resource for unlocking assets and building resilience in communities. Community Development Journal 2013;48(1):134-150.

Campell-Sills L, Stein MB. Psychometric analysis and refinement of the Connor-Davidson Resilience Scale (CDRISC): Validation of a 10 item measure of resilience. Journal of Traumatic Stress 2007;20(6):1019-1028.

Castro FG, Murray, KE. Cultural Adaptation and Resilience: Controversies, issues and Emerging Models. In: Reich, Zautra and Hall (eds.) Handbook of Adult Resilience. New York: The Guilford Press; 2010.

Centers for Disease Control and Prevention (CDC) Geospatial Research A& SP (GRASP). CDC's Social Vulnerability Index (SVI) 2016 Documentation. (2018). p. 1–24. Available online at: https://svi.cdc.gov/data-and-tools-download.html

Chan C, Chan T, Ng S. The strength-focused and meaning-oriented approach to resilience and transformation (SMART). Social Work in Health Care 2006;43(2-3):9-36.

Chapin R, Cox EO. Changing the paradigm: strengths-based and empowerment-oriented social work with frail elders. Journal of Gerontological Social Work 2002;36(3-4):165-179.

Christopherson S, Michie J, Tyler P. Regional resilience: theoretical and empirical perspectives. Cambridge Journal of Regions, Economy and Society 2010;3(1):3-10.

Connor KM, Davidson JRT. Development of a new resilience scale: the Connor-Davidson Resilience Scale (CD-RISC). Depression and Anxiety 2003;18(2):76-82.

Daniel B, Wassell S. Adolescence: Assessing and promoting resilience in vulnerable children. London: Jessica Kingsley Publishers; 2002.

Dobson J. Community infrastructure still critical to new housing in localist era. York: Joseph Rowntree Foundation; 2011.

Donnon T, Hammond W, Charles G. Youth resiliency: assessing students' capacity for success at school. Teaching and Learning 2003;1(2):23-28.

Donnon T, Hammond W. A psychometric assessment of the self-reported youth resiliency: assessing developmental strengths questionnaire. Psychological Reports 2007;100(3 Pt 1):963-978.

Ehrenreich B. Smile or die: How positive thinking fooled America and the world. London: Granta Books; 2010.

Edwards C. Resilient nation. London: Demos; 2009.

Erikson, K. Everything in its Path (Simon and Schuster, 1976).

Experian. The Insight Report. An Experian report – Quarter 4, 2009. Nottingham: Experian; 2009.

Ezzy D. Unemployment and mental health: a critical review. Social Science & Medicine 1993;37(1):41-52.

Feinstein L, Hammond C. The contribution of adult learning to health and social capital. Oxford Review of Education 2004;30(2):199-221.

Findlay S, Pereira I, Fryer-Smith E, Charlton A, Roberts-Hughes R. The way we live now. Ipsos Mori and RIBA; 2012.

Friborg O, Hjemdal O, Rosenvinge JH, Martinussen M. A new rating scale for adult resilience: What are the central protective resources behind healthy adjustment? International Journal of Methods in Psychiatric Research 2003;12(2):65-76.

Friedli L. Always look on the bright side: The rise of asset based approached in Scotland. Scottish Anti Poverty Review Winter 2011/12;(issue 14):11-15.

Furstenberg F, Cook T, Eccles J, Elder G, Sameroff A. Managing to make it: Urban families and adolescent success. Chicago: University of Chicago Press; 1999.

Future Communities. Amenities and social infrastructure. https://arc.aarpinternational.org/File%20Library/Full%20Reports/ARC-Report---Community-Social-Infrastructure.pdf

Gans, H. Planning, social : I I Regional and urban. I n D. Sills (d .), International encyclopedia of the social sciences. Vol . 1 2 . pp. 1 29-1 3 7 . New York: Macmillan and Free Press, 1 968.

Garmezy N. Children in poverty: Resilience despite risk. Psychiatry 1993;56(1):127-136.

Gilligan R. Beyond permanence? The importance of resilience in child placement practice and planning. Adoption and Fostering 1997;21(1):12-20.

Gilligan R. Promoting resilience: A resource guide on working with children in the care system. London: British Agencies for Adoption and Fostering; 2001.

Gilligan R. Promoting a sense of 'secure base' for children in foster care – Exploring the potential contribution of foster fathers. Journal of Social Work Practice 2012;26(4):473-486.

Glover J. Bouncing back: How can resilience be promoted in vulnerable children and young people? Ilford: Barnardo's: 2009.

Godschalk D. Urban hazard mitigation: Creating resilient cities. Natural Hazards Review 2003;4(3):136-143.

Graham H, Power C. Childhood disadvantage and health inequalities: a framework for policy based on life course research. Child Care: Health and Development 2004;30(6):671-678.

Granovetter M. The strength of weak ties: A network theory revisited. Sociological Theory 1983;1(1):201-233.

Grotberg E. A Guide to Promoting Resilience in Children: Strengthening the Human Spirit. University of Illinois; 1995.

Hammond C. Impacts of lifelong learning upon emotional resilience, psychological and mental health: fieldwork evidence. Oxford Review of Education 2004;30(4):551-568.

Hanlon P, Carlisle S, Reilly D, Lyon A, Hannah M. Enabling well-being in a time of radical change: Integrative public health for the 21st century. Public Health 2010;124:305-312.

Harkins C, Egan J. The rise of in-work poverty and the changing nature of poverty and work in Scotland, – what are the implications for population health and wellbeing? Glasgow: GCPH; 2013.

Harper S, Lynch J, Hsu W-L et al. Life course socioeconomic conditions and adult psychosocial functioning. Int J Epidemiol 2002;31:395–403

Harrop E, Addis S, Elliott E, Williams G. Resilience, coping and salutogenic approaches to maintaining and generating health: a review. Cardiff: Cardiff University; 2006.

Hayslip J, Smith G. Resilience in Adulthood and later Life: what does it mean and where are we heading? Annual Review of Gerontology and Geriatrics 2012;32:1-28.

Hill M, Stafford A, Seaman P, Ross N. Daniel B. Parenting and Resilience. York: Joseph Rowntree Foundation; 2007.

Hjemdal O, Friborg O, Stiles TC, Martinussen M, Rosenvinge JH. A new scale for adolescent resilience: grasping the central protective resources behind healthy development. Measurement and Evaluation in Counseling and Development 2003;39:98-96.

Holling CS. Resilience and stability of ecological systems. Annual Review of Ecology and Systematics 1973;4:1-23.

Holling CS. Understanding the complexity of economic, ecological, and social systems. Ecosystems 2001;4(5):390-405.

Holling CS, Gunderson LH. Resilience and Adaptive Cycles. In: Gunderson LH, Holling CS (eds.) Panarchy: Understanding Transformations in Human and Natural Systems. Washington, DC: Island Press; 2001. p27-33.

Jacobs J. The death and life of great American cities. New York: Vintage; 1961.

Jahoda M. Economic recession and mental health: Some conceptual issues. Journal of Social Issues 1988;44(4):13-23.

Johnson Vickberg SM. Fears about breast cancer recurrence: Interviews with a diverse sample. Cancer Practice 2001;9(5):237-243.

Jones C, Shao B. The net generation and digital natives: implications for higher education. York: Higher Education Academy; 2011.

Joseph DH, Griffin M, Hall RF, Sullivan ED: Peer coaching: an intervention for individuals struggling with diabetes. Diabetes Educ 27:703–710, 2001

Kawachi, C. The relationship between health assets, social capital and cohesive communities. In: Morgan A, Davies M, Ziglio E (eds.) Health assets in a global context: theory, methods, action. New York: Springer; 2010.

Kendall E, Del Fabbro L, Ehrlich C, Rixon K. Rebuilding community: considerations for policy makers in the wake of the 2011 Queensland floods. Australian Health Review 2011;35(4):520-522.

E. Klinenberg, Heat Wave: A Social Autopsy of Disaster in Chicago (University of Chicago Press, 2015).

Klohnen EC. Conceptual analysis and measurement of the construct of ego-resiliency. Journal of Personality and Social Psychology 1996;70:1067-1079.

Kumpfer K, Bluth B. Parent/child transactional processes predictive of resilience or vulnerability to "substance abuse disorders". Substance Use & Misuse 2004;39(5):671-698.

Landau J, Weaver AM. The LINC model of family and community resilience: New approaches to disaster response. Journal of Family and Consumer Sciences 2006;98(2):11-14.

Lebel L, Anderies JM, Cambell B, Folke C, Hatfield-Dodds S, Hughes TP, Wilson J. Governance and the capacity to manage resilience in regional social-ecological systems. Ecology and Society 2006;11(1):19.

Lin KK, Sandler IN, Ayers TS, Wolchik SA, Luecken LJ. Resilience in parentally bereaved children and adolescents seeking preventive services. Journal of Clinical Child and Adolescent Psychology 2004;33(4):673-683.

Luthar SS, Cicchetti D. The construct of resilience: implications for interventions and social policies. Development and Psychopathology 2000;12(4):587-885.

Luthar SS, Zelazo LB. Research on resilience: An integrative review. In: Luthar SS (ed.) Resilience and vulnerability: Adaptation in the context of childhood adversities. Cambridge: Cambridge University Press; 2003. p510- 549.

Lynch J, Davey Smith G, Harper S, Hillemeier M, Ross N, Kaplan GA, et al. Is income inequality a determinant of population health? Part 1: a systematic review. Milbank Quarterly 2004;82(1):5-99.

Lynch J, Kaplan G. Socioeconomic position. In: Berkman LF, Kawachi I, editors. Social epidemiology. New York: Oxford University Press, 2000:13-35.

Marmot M. Wilkinson R. Social determinants of health. New York; Oxford University Press; 2006.

Lynch JW, Kaplan GA, Shema SJ. Cumulative impact of sustained economic hardship on physical, cognitive, psychological, and social functioning. New England Journal of Medicine 1997;337(26):1889-1895.

P. B. Maffetone, P. B. Laursen, The perfect storm: Coronavirus (Covid-19) pandemic meets overfat pandemic. Front. Public Health 8, 135 (2020).

Martin-Breen P, Anderies M. Resilience: A literature review. New York: City University of New York, and Arizona State University; 2011.

Masten AS, Coatsworth JD. The development of competence in favorable and unfavorable environments: Lessons from research on successful children. American Psychologist 1998;53(2):205.

Masten AS, Powell JL. A resilience framework for research, policy, and practice. In: Luthar SS (ed.) Resilience and vulnerability: Adaptation in the context of childhood adversities: Cambridge: Cambridge University Press; 2003. p1-25.

Matarasso F. Use or ornament? The social impact of participation in the arts. London: Comedia Publishing Group; 1997.

McGuinness D, McGlynn L, Johnson PCD, MacIntyre A, Batty GD, Burns H, Cavanagh J, Deans KA, Ford I, McConnachie A, McGinty A, McLean JS, Millar K, Packard CJ, Sattar N, Tannahill C, Velupillai YN, Shiels PG. Socio- economic status is associated with epigenetic differences in the pSoBid cohort. International Journal of Epidemiology 2012;41(1):151-160.

MacKinnon D, Derickson K. From resilience to resourcefulness: A critique of resilience policy and activism. Progress in Human Geography 2012;37(2):253- 270.

Massey,D.S. Categorically Unequal: The American Stratification System (Russell Sage Foundation, 2007).

Mguni N, Bacon N. Taking the temperature of local communities: The Wellbeing and Resilience Measure (WARM). London: The Young Foundation; 2010.

Mguni N, Caistor-Arendar L. Rowing against the tide. Making the case for community resilience. London: The Young Foundation; 2012.

Morse SW. Smart communities: How citizens and local leaders can use strategic thinking to build a brighter future. San Francisco: Jossey-Bass Publishers; 2004.

Moser CO. Ordinary families, extraordinary lives: Assets and poverty reduction in Guayaquil, 1978-2004. Washington, DC: Brookings Institute Press; 2009.

Newman T, Yates T, Masten A. What Works in Building Resilience?

Barkingside: Barnardo's; 2004.

Newman P, Beatley T, Boyer H. Resilient cities: responding to peak oil and climate change. Washington DC: Island Press; 2009.

Newman J, Barnes M, Sullivan H, Knops A. Public participation and

collaborative governance. J Soc Policy. 2004;33(02):203–23.

Olsson CA, Bond L, Burns JM, Vella-Brodrick DA, Sawyer SM. Adolescent resilience: a concept analysis. Journal of Adolescence 2003;26(1):1-11.

Olsson P, Gunderson LH, Carpenter SR, Ryan P, Lebel L, Folke C, Holling CS. Shooting the Rapids: Navigating Transitions to Adaptive Governance of Social-Ecological Systems. Ecology and Society 2006;11(1):18.

Oshio A, Kaneko H, Nagamine S, Nakaya M. Construct validity of the Adolescent Resilience Scale. Psychological Reports 2003;93(3 Pt 2):1217-1222.

Ostrom E. Crafting institutions for self-governing irrigation systems. San Francisco: Institute for Contemporary Studies Press; 1992.

Oxford English Compact Dictionary Online. Entry for infrastructure. http://oxforddictionaries.com/definition/english/infrastructure

Oxford English Dictionary Online. Entry for resilience. http://www.oed.com/view/Entry/163619?redirectedFrom=resilience#eid

Pawson R, Tilley N. Realistic evaluation. London: Sage Publications; 1997.

Paxson,C, Fussell, E Rhodes,J Waters,M Five years later: Recovery from post-traumatic stress and psychological distress among low-income mothers affected by Hurricane Katrina. Soc. Sci. Med. 74, 150–157 (2012).

Pertrillo AS, Prosperi DC. Metaphors from the Resilience Literature: Guidance for Planners. In: Schrenk M, Popovich VV, Zeile P (eds.) Proceedings of REAL CORP 2011 (16th International Conference on Urban Planning, Regional Development and Information Society); 2011. p601-611.

Pinnock K, Evans R. Developing responsive preventative practices: key messages from children's and families' experiences of the Children's Fund. Children and Society 2008;22(2):86-98.

Power, C., & Manor, O. (1992). Explaining social class differences in psychological health among young adults: a longitudinal perspective. Social Psychiatry & Psychiatric Epidemiology, 27, 284e291

Redbird, B, Grusky,D. B. Distributional effects of the great recession: Where has all the sociology gone? Annu. Rev. Sociol. 42, 185–215 (2016).

Reich JW, Zautra A, Hall JS. Handbook of Adult Resilience. New York: Guilford Press; 2010.

Rutter M. Resilience concepts and findings: implications for family therapy.

Journal of Family Therapy 1999;21(2):119-144.

Sabates R. The impact of lifelong learning on poverty reduction. Leicester: National Institute of Adult and Continuing Education (NIACE): 2008.

Schuller T, Brassett-Grundy A, Green A, Hammond C, Preston J. Learning, continuity and change in adult life. Wider Benefits of Learning Research Report Number 3. London: Centre for Research on the Wider Benefits of Learning; 2002.

Schumpeter JA. Capitalism, socialism and democracy. New York: Harper & Row; 1950.

Sennett R. The Corrosion of Character: The Personal Consequences of Work in the New Capitalism. New York: Norton; 1998.

Smith BW, Dalen J, Wiggins K, Tooley E, Christopher P, Bernard J. The brief resilience scale: assessing the ability to bounce back. International Journal of Behavioral Medicine 2008;15(3):194-200.

Smith-Osborne A, Whitehall Bolton K. Assessing resilience: A review of measures across the life course. Journal of Evidence-Based Social Work 2013;10(2):111-126.

Sonn C, Fisher A. Sense of community: Community resilient responses to oppression and change. Journal of Community Psychology 1998;26(5):401-508.

Standing G. The Precariat: A New Dangerous Class. London: Bloomsbury; 2011.

Sterns HL, Dawson NT. Emerging Perspectives on Resilience in Adulthood and Later Life: Work, Retirement, and Resilience. Annual Review of Gerontology and Geriatrics 2012;32(1):211-230.

Sun J, Stewart D. Development of population-based resilience measures in the primary school setting. Health Education 2007;107(6):575-599.

Terwee CB, Bot SD, de Boer MR, van der Windt DA, Knol DL, Dekker J, Bouter LM, de Vet HC. Quality criteria were proposed for measurement properties of health status questionnaires. Journal of Clinical Epidemiology 2007;60(1):34-42.

Tilly C. Durable inequality. Berkeley: University of California Press; 1999.

Thompson, L. The Secret of Culture: The Nine Communities Study. New York: Random House; 1969.

Ungar, M. Researching and theorizing resilience across contexts. Preventive Medicine 2012;55(5):387-389.

Vanderbilt-Adriance E, Shaw DS. Conceptualizing and re-evaluating resilience across levels of risk, time, and domains of competence. Clinical Child and Family Psychology Review 2008;11(1-2):30-58.

Waddell G, Burton AK. Is work good for your health and well-being? London: The Stationery Office: 2006.

Walker J, Cooper M. Genealogies of resilience: from systems ecology to the political economy of crisis adaptation. Security Dialogue 2011;42(2):143-160.

Walker B, Salt D. Resilience thinking: sustaining ecosystems and people in a changing world. Washington, DC: Island Press; 2006.

Walsh F. Beliefs, spirituality, and transcendence: Keys to family resilience. In: McGoldrick M (ed.) Re-visioning family therapy: Race, culture, and gender in clinical practice. New York: Guilford Press; 1998. p62-77.

Warhurst C. Rethinking good and bad jobs in Glasgow: A Whose Economy

Seminar Paper; 2011.

Warr PB. Work, unemployment, and mental health. Oxford: Clarendon Press; 1987.

Waters, M.C. Life after Hurricane Katrina: The resilience in survivors of Katrina (RISK) Project. Soc. Forum 31, 750–769.

Werner EE. Protective factors and individual resilience. In: Shonkoff JP, Meisels SJ (eds.) Handbook of Early Childhood Intervention. Cambridge: Cambridge University Press; 1990. p97-116.

Werner EE, Johnson J. Can we apply resilience? In: Glantz M and Johnson JL (eds.) Resilience and Development: Positive Life Adaptations. New York: Kluwer Acaedmic/Plenum Publishers; 1999.

Werner EE, Smith RS. Overcoming the Odds: High Risk Children from Birth to Adulthood. Ithaca, NY: Cornell University Press; 1993.

White, M. 1995: 'Reflecting teamwork as definitional ceremony.' In Re-Authoring Lives: Interviews and essays, pp.172-198. Adelaide: Dulwich Centre Publications.

White M. 2000: Reflections on Narrative Practice: Essays and interviews. Adelaide: Dulwich Centre Publications.

Wilber K. A theory of everything: an integral vision for business, politics, science and spirituality. Dublin: Gateway; 2001

Wilding N. Exploring Community Resilience. Dunfermline: Carnegie UK Trust; 2011.

Wilkinson R, Marmot M, editors. The solid facts : social determinants of health. 2nd ed. Copenhagen: Centre for Urban Health, World Health Organization, 2003.

Windle G. Critical conceptual and measurement issues in the study of resilience. In: Glantz M, Johnston JL (eds.) Resilience and Development: Positive Life Adaptations.. New York: Kluwer Acaedmic/Plenum Publishers; 1999.

Windle G, Markland DA, Woods RT. Examination of a theoretical model of psychological resilience in older age. Aging & Mental Health 2008;12(3):285- 292.

Windle G, Bennett KM, Noyes J. A methodological review of resilience measurement scales. Health and Quality of Life Outcomes 2011;9:8.

Woolcock M. Social capital and economic development: Toward a theoretical synthesis and policy framework. Theory and Society 1998;27(2):151-208.

Young OR. Institutional dynamics: resilience, vulnerability and adaptation in environmental and resource regimes. Global Environmental Change 2010;20(3):378-385.

Zautra AJ, Hall JS, Murray KE. Resilience: A new definition of Health for People and Communities. In: Reich, Zautra and Hall (eds.) Handbook of Adult Resilience. New York: Guilford Press; 2010